Sad-Face Clown

Emmett Kelly

D1521385

Sad-Face Clown: Emmett Kelly is part of THE GREAT HEARTLANDERS SERIES. This collection of biographies for children describes the lives of local heroes – men and women of all races and careers – who have made lasting contributions to the nation and the world.

SAD-FACE CLOWN:
Emmett Kelly

Copyright © 2004 by Acorn Books

Acorn Books
7337 Terrace
Kansas City, MO 64114

Cataloging-in-Publication Data
J.L. Wilkerson
Sad-Face Clown: Emmett Kelly / by J. L. Wilkerson
Library of Congress Control Number: 2003102744
Series Title: The Great Heartlanders Series
ISBN 0-9664470-9-3
1. Emmett Kelly, 1898-1979 - Juvenile literature.
2. Kansas - Missouri - Ringling Bros. & Barnum Bailey
Circus - Circus - Clown - Great Britain - Biography -
History - Juvenile literature - Midwest.

10 9 8 7 6 5 4 3 2 1

Dedication

For all the friends and supporters of THE GREAT HEARTLANDERS SERIES who understand the importance of providing children the opportunity to learn about their local heroes.

Acknowledgements

Appreciation to Jim Mordy for his inspired suggestion to create a book about Emmett Kelly.

Gratitude to John and Nancy Floyd, and Shirley Boulanger of Sedan, Kansas, for their hospitality and help during the research of the Kelly book.

Thanks to Betty Dixon for her careful attention to detail.

Book production by Acorn Books, Kansas City, Missouri.

Image Credits:
Circus World Museum: page 64 and 74.
Ralph L. Emerson, Jr.: page 94.
Hartford Courant: pages 97 and 98.
Kansas City, Missouri, Public Library, Special Collections: page 28.
Library of Congress: pages 42, 44, 48 and 50.
United States National Archives and Records Administration: pages 16, 26, and 87.
Universal Film Studio: pages 104-105.
Wisconsin Historical Society: page 62.

Contents

I am a sad and ragged little guy who is very serious about everything he attempts – no matter how futile or how foolish it appears to be. I am the hobo who found out the hard way that the deck is stacked, the dice 'frozen,' the race fixed and the wheel crooked, but there is always present that one tiny, forlorn spark of hope still glimmering in his soul which makes him keep on trying. All I can say beyond that is that there must be a lot of people in this world who feel that way and that, fortunately, they come to the circus. In my tramp clown character, folks who are down on their luck, have had disappointments and have maybe been pushed around by circumstances beyond their control, see a caricature of themselves. By laughing at me, they really laugh at themselves, and realizing that they have done this gives them a sort of spiritual second wind for going back into the battle.

From *Clown*, Emmett Kelly's autobiography.

1

Booming, Razzing, Blaring, Trilling

Emmett Kelly bent his head to one side. He listened. Except for his mother, humming in the kitchen, all was silent. And yet he was sure he heard the sound.

Emmett turned an ear toward the open front door. He waited.

Yes, there it was. That sound – like a far-off cannonball dropped from the sky. The deep boom seemed to rise up from the ground. Emmett felt it in his feet, in his chest. A moment of silence followed, and then again – boom, boom, boom!

Emmett recognized the sound. A tuba.

The Saturday evening concert had started. Just a few blocks away, in the center of Sedan, Kansas, the band was playing its opening march.

Emmett had promised to watch his little sister, Sylvia, while his mother finished churning the butter on the back porch. All afternoon, Emmett had looked after the two-year-old. He fed her. He played with her. And just in the nick of time, he stopped her from eating a potato bug.

Emmett stepped to the front door. Mixed with the boom-boom-boom, the faint razzing sound of a trombone drifted past. He took Sylvia's hand and led her to the front yard. Couldn't he watch his sister in the yard as easily as in the house? Of course he could, Emmett said to himself. True, his mother had told him to "stay within earshot." But surely Emmett could hear her from the yard.

Just last summer, his mother had spanked Emmett for the first time. He had climbed to the top of a telephone pole. Half the neighborhood came to see him.

"Quite a stunt for a five-year-old," one man said, looking up at Emmett perched on the crossarm.

"Stunt, indeed," Emmett's mother said. She stood with her hands on her hips and her eyes as narrow as a cat whisker. Wasn't it enough that almost daily the boy ran off to play in the railroad yard? His father or another rail yard worker was forever hauling Emmett from under a train. She

2

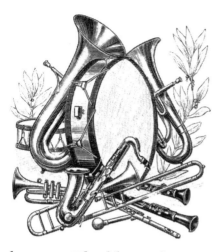

was a patient woman, but the telephone pole was the limit.

Emmett remembered the spanking, and he didn't want another. He made up his mind to obey his mother – to watch his sister and stay within earshot.

Emmett stood by the gate. The blare of a trumpet shot through the air. Razz went the trombone. Boom went the tuba. The sounds faded as a wagonload of teenaged boys rattled by. They, too, were headed to town for the concert.

Emmett looked toward the house. Maybe he'd stand in the street, where he could hear the band better. Surely there wasn't any harm in that. In the street, he would still be within earshot of his mother. Emmett grabbed Sylvia's hand and headed out the gate.

The sharp trill of a piccolo flitted by like a flock of canaries. Little pieces of John Phillips Sousa's "The Stars and Stripes Forever" pounded out the beat of a military march. Without even noticing, Emmett began walking toward the sound. The booming, razzing, blaring and trilling pulled him forward. By the time he realized what was happening, he and Sylvia were half way to town.

Emmett looked back. Was he within earshot? If his mother stood in the middle of the street and yelled at the top of her lungs, Emmett would hear her – surely.

Punishment

Emmett lay in bed. He heard his parents talking in the kitchen downstairs. This was his seventh night to go directly to his room after dinner. His mother hadn't spanked him. One week without playing after supper – that was his punishment. The worst was tonight. Saturday. The night of the weekly concert.

Through the open window he heard the music drift from town. The liquid-gold sound of the brass instruments invaded his room, teasing him to follow. In his mind, he could see the band conductor, waving his baton in graceful whirls. Perched on the bandstand, the musicians wore white uniforms trimmed in gold braid. Their instruments gleamed.

How did a fellow, Emmett asked himself, become a musician? Maybe that's what he would do when he grew up. What a wonder that would be!

From below in the kitchen, Emmett heard his father's voice. Last Thursday Mr. Kelly celebrated his birthday. That event always inspired him to talk about his job. He worked as section foreman for the Missouri Pacific Railroad. The company retired its employees at the age of 65. Every birthday reminded Mr. Kelly of the forced retirement looming ahead. He swore he'd never let the company "fire" him.

"I'll quit first!" his father said.

Born in Ireland, Mr. Kelly came to the United States at the age of 21. He lived for a while in New York City and then moved west to work on the railroads. Mr. Kelly was more than 40 years old when he met Emmett's mother, who was only 18 years old. Her family, immigrants from Bohemia, disapproved of their romance. And so the couple eloped.

Emmett heard the faint sound of a whistle. The evening train from Kansas City was coming in. The far-off whistle blended with the drifting notes of the brass band. Were there any sweeter sounds in all the world than brass bands and trains?

In the kitchen, Emmett's mother counted out the money from the sugar jar. It was money she earned by selling her butter. Missouri-Pacific paid Mr. Kelly one dollar a day. Every week he set aside a portion of his earnings. Together he and Mrs. Kelly were saving to buy a farm.

The whistle sounded again, this time much

louder. Emmett judged the Kansas City train was just beyond the ridge north of town. Sedan, Kansas, lay in a shallow valley surrounded by low hills. That was why Emmett had climbed the telephone pole – to see what lay beyond those hills. He hadn't seen Kansas City. And though he twisted around in the opposite direction, he hadn't even seen the Oklahoma Territory. All Emmett could see, for miles and miles in any direction, was just the broad expanse of ranch land.

A long blare of the whistle announced that the Kansas City train was rolling into the station. Right about now, Emmett's father would pull out his big Waltham pocketwatch and check to see that the Kansas City train was on time. It always was. Then Mr. Kelly would stand, take his hat from the peg by the door and walk to the train station.

Since spring began, Emmett loved listening to Sedan's brass band. But the sounds of trains had been part of his life for as long as he could remember. He rarely went to sleep without those sounds – the lonely whistles, clicking wheels, and rolling cars. He hoped his father wasn't serious about leaving the railroad company. How would Emmett fall asleep at night on a farm?

Twenty minutes later, the whistle blew again. Emmett heard the hiss of the steam engine and the

slow chug as the locomotive began to lurch forward. Maybe he'd be a railroad man when he grew up. He'd throw switches, pull levers and every hour on the hour he'd pull out the biggest Waltham watch in the county. What a wonder that would be!

3

The Farm

Mr. Kelly was true to his word. A few months later and several years before retirement age, he quit his railroad job. With their savings, Mr. and Mrs. Kelly made a down payment on a farm in Texas County, Missouri.

The farmhouse wasn't ready when the Kellys arrived in Missouri, and the family lived for a while in a tent. The farm, the tent, the neighbors – it was all too new and strange for Emmett and his sister, Sylvia. They cried themselves to sleep each night, longing for their old house and friends in Kansas.

The family moved to Missouri in the spring, at plowing time. Shortly after they arrived, Mr. Kelly became sick. Emmett watched his father, pale and listless, on his cot in the back of the tent. Mr. Kelly was too weak to work in the fields. Seven-year-old Emmett would have to plow the 80-acres.

Emmett's hands could barely grip the plow handles. The big horse pulling the plow loomed ahead of him like the backend of a Missouri-Pacific locomotive. Every time Emmett managed to push the heavy blade into the hard ground, the horse bolted forward and yanked the boy up and over the plow handles. By late afternoon, the family realized they were in trouble.

Emmett's muscles were so sore that during supper he could barely lift his arms. His mother stood at the tent's door flap, staring sadly at the one – and only – row Emmett had plowed. Sylvia asked if this meant the family would move back to Kansas. Emmett nodded hopefully.

Mrs. Kelly suddenly cupped her hand above her eyes, as if trying to see something in the distance. "What do you suppose…?" she asked.

Emmett, joining her at the door, watched as a farmer and a team of horses came through the gate. Without a word, the man and his horses headed into the Kelly's unplowed field. Right behind him was another farmer and horses …and another…and another. Before long a half dozen men and their plow teams were working the field. Shortly after sundown, the farm was plowed.

Nobody talked of moving back to Kansas again.

Snakes and Balloons

Emmett looked up at the sky. It was a dome of pale blue, as if bleached from the long hot days of August. A single cloud hovered above the pond. Gray as old dishwater, the cloud hung there, threatening rain.

Rain.

Please, thought Emmett, not today. No rain. If the land were as dry as a snake's skin, Emmett would have wished for sun. If the pond were an empty hole or the crops lay withered in the fields, Emmett would have wished for a cloudless sky.

Because today was the Old Settler's Reunion. It was the county's biggest annual carnival. Two years ago Emmett saw his first automobile at the Reunion. Every August, Emmett and Sylvia hoped for good weather on this day. For weeks they saved their pennies and nickels. And when the day came, they dressed in their best clothes. Emmett's ears and neck still burned from this morning's scrubbing.

The smell of fried chicken came from the kitchen. Mrs. Kelly was packing the box lunch. Biscuits, potato salad, peaches and chicken – a perfect picnic for the trip to town.

Mr. Kelly emerged from the house. Emmett's heart leaped. His father would now decide whether the weather was good enough to go to the Reunion. Emmett had high hopes. Already this week was proving lucky. His teacher had seen him drawing in class, making sketches of trains and Model As. When Emmett drew them, he imagined himself traveling through the far-off countries he was studying in school. Last Monday, his teacher told his parents about the drawings. She said they were good, and that Mr. and Mrs. Kelly should encourage him.

Today, Mr. Kelly looked at the lone cloud above the pond. He licked his finger and raised it in the air. "No wind," he said, and turned to Emmett. "No rain."

This was, indeed, turning into Emmett's lucky week.

The wagon bounced along the four miles to Houston, Missouri. With each mile, the road became increasingly crowded with families heading to the Reunion. The growing clatter of wagons and shouts from friends added to Emmett and Sylvia's excitement.

Before the wheels rolled to a stop at the Reunion's fairgrounds, Emmett jumped from the buckboard. Before noon, Emmett rode the merry-go-round so many times that he lost count. He ate popcorn and rock candy until his jaws ached. He and his friends bought bags of confetti and threw them at girls. Emmett bought a Singing Balloon, which made a strange fluttering noise as air escaped across a thin reed. He saw a two-headed calf, a

bearded lady, and a sword swallower. And four times he watched a man named Snakoid eat foot-long garden snakes.

The man announcing the snake act said, "Men, women, ladies and gentlemen – right this way to see Snakoid, the only man in the world who swallows snakes alive right before your eyes – or we will give you your money back."

Watching the snake man was certainly fun, but the real fun was watching the audience. With rapt attention, the people stared up at Snakoid on the little platform in front of a red curtain. The man held back his head and raised the wriggling snake above his mouth. The crowd gasped. Snakoid slowly lowered the snake into his open mouth. A few people covered their eyes. When Snakoid closed his mouth, his checks puffed out, as if the trapped snake were struggling to escape. Many in the audience giggled nervously. The head of the snake poked out of the man's mouth. Its forked tongue danced about. Snakoid sucked the head back inside and instantly gulped loudly. Some people grabbed their throats. One woman fainted. When the applause and whistles began to fade, Snakoid quickly disappeared behind the small, red curtain.

The worst part of the day came when Emmett's mother called the children to the wagon. Time to go home. The family always left before sundown.

Not far from the fairgrounds, Mr. Kelly pulled the wagon beside a creek. The family looked back for a glimpse of the last event of the day: the balloon ascension. Brightly painted yellow and red, the balloon rose slowly. A daredevil dangled from a swing underneath. People on the ground craned their necks to see. Now high above the trees – even higher than ten telephone poles stacked end on end – the man let go of the swing. The crowd gasped. Almost immediately, a parachute opened and the man floated gently toward the ground, waving at the people below.

That evening, when he was in bed, Emmett imagined himself swallowing swords and eating snakes – giant snakes, big as copperheads. He imagined himself perched on top of a pole – so tall that the people on the ground looked like pinheads in a pincushion. He could see all the way to Oklahoma and Kansas City. On the pole, Emmett stood on his head. He balanced on one foot, and then to

15

the wonderment of the pinheads below, he did a complete and perfect backflip.

Maybe he would be a carnival daredevil when he grew up. What a wonder that would be!

Just as Emmett drifted off to sleep, he heard a train whistle far in the distance. He hadn't heard that sound in months. He took it for a very good sign.

A hundred years ago, dozens of small circuses traveled around the United States, performing in or near small towns. They were called "mud shows" because they toured the hills and backroads of America. The first circus Emmett saw, the Mighty Haag Show, was a mud show. Called the Hog Show by circus people, it was one of the oldest circuses in the country.

In his autobiography, Emmett wrote, "Probably it would make a good story if I said that when I saw my first circus I immediately had a desire to be a clown. It wouldn't be true. Even when I finally took off after the red wagons, I never meant to be a clown. My ambition as a kid and as a young man and, even now, has been to be an artist."

5

The Chalk-Talk Cartoonist

One day when Emmett came in from evening chores, Mrs. Kelly set a cardboard box in front of him. The return address on the mailing label said, "Landon School of Cartooning in Cleveland, Ohio." Inside were drawing paper, pencils and an artist's lesson book. Emmett's mother had paid $25 for the correspondence course. Twenty-five lessons – a dollar a lesson.

Emmett followed each lesson: drawing the assigned cartoon and then mailing it to Ohio for review. He started with fruits – apples and pears, mostly – and then worked up to animals and finally people.

On the sixth week – "Lesson: Large Animals" – Emmett sat on a fence drawing Charlie, the family's old horse. Charlie was certainly large, but more importantly, he was still. Occasionally his back

muscle twitched, but mostly Charlie had as much energy as a turnip. That made him a perfect specimen to sketch for lesson six.

Suddenly, as if hit by buckshot, Charlie threw back his head and bolted for the barn. Emmett heard a low rumble and looked toward the road.

An old yellow box wagon, pulled by four mules, drove past the farm. More wagons followed. Stenciled across each were the words, "The Mighty Haag Circus and All Feature Show."

Emmett had heard of circuses but had never seen one. Painted on the wagons were wild animals. Giant Bengal tigers crouched threateningly, their white teeth bared. Prancing horses carried ballerinas standing on tiptoe.

Behind the fourth wagon, an elephant, its feet wrapped in gunnysacks, tramped along. Emmett could hardly believe his eyes. Next came a cage on wheels – inside was a tiger. The final wagon in the caravan had a camel hitched to the end.

That evening, the Mighty Haag Circus pitched

its tent at a crossroads. By the time Emmett arrived to see his first circus, the tent was filled with local farmers and townspeople.

Emmett also saw his first clown that night. A short, slender man, the clown wore the traditional "whiteface" clown costume. Almost everything on his body was white. His loose-fitting shirt and stiff pantaloons were brilliant white. He wore white gloves and shoes. A white scull cap covered his head. Except for tiny, bright red lips and thick black lines surrounding his eyes, the clown's face and neck were painted white.

Afterwards, Emmett couldn't stop thinking about the Haag Circus. Not even the Old Settlers Reunion compared to the dazzle of the circus. Emmett figured the Mighty Haag was a once-in-a-lifetime experience, until two days later when he saw posters announcing another circus. This one – the M. L. Clark and Sons Combined Shows – was much bigger than the Haag show.

The Clark circus performed under a big top with two rings. Right after the bucking mule perfor-mance ended in the first ring, the juggling act started in the second ring. That way the show never stopped. When the jugglers finished, two clowns performed in the first ring. Back and forth – acro-bats followed bareback riding, trained dogs fol-lowed the cloud swing act. The swing act was an aerialist who spun and sailed through the air over the audience.

The highlight was the trapeze act. Hanging by his knees from a bar, an aerialist held the ankles of a slender woman. Across the ring, swinging from a second bar, a third aerialist swung out just as the woman leaped through the air toward him. The audience was on their feet. Would the woman fall to her death?

Emmett stopped breathing. He thought of the snake man. Eating snakes was certainly shocking, even wonderfully disgusting, but it was not life threatening. In the next instant the woman might land, a mangled wreck, on the ground. But in that next instant, with death just an eye blink away, the third aerialist reached out and snatched the woman's hands.

It was beautiful. Amazing. Stupendous. Emmett couldn't think of enough words to describe the thrill of the circus. Years later, he wrote, "As I walked away I looked back and wondered where it had

come from and where it was going. The farm seemed far away. Something that later caught fire in me was stirring that night. But I was a farm boy and school was starting and I had to go home."

The pages of his sketchbook began filling with images of zebras, elephants and camels. In week twenty of his correspondence course, when the task was to draw people, his book filled with jugglers, clowns and flying trapeze artists.

Emmett wondered if he could earn a living working as a circus painter. Maybe he could sign on with one of the local shows. He recently heard that Lancaster and Rolla, Missouri, and Quenemo, Kansas, were headquarters for some national circuses.

Shortly after seeing the Clark circus, Emmett found a library book by a man named Guy Lockwood. The book described how to entertain people while drawing cartoons. At that time, "chalk-talk" was a popular form of entertainment. A chalk-talk artist got the name of someone in the audience and then wrote that name on an easel. With a few strokes of the pen, the artist turned the letters of the name into a drawing – maybe a portrait of that person, or a motor car or a bouquet of roses. With just a handful of letters, a good chalk-talk artist could sketch anything – quickly and easily.

Maybe Emmett could work as a chalk-talk artist, he thought. He imagined himself performing at the Old Settler's Reunion. The entire county would gasp at his brilliant drawing techniques and laugh at his witty jokes.

In the barn, Emmett set up an easel with several blank pieces of paper. Every Sunday afternoon, he practiced his chalk-talk routine. Everyone in the barn watched. Charlie and Dan (the family's other horse) quietly ate from their troughs and stared at Emmett. He turned Charlie's name into the head of a mule. He turned Dan's name into the Man-in-the-Moon.

One day, shortly before Thanksgiving, Emmett's teacher asked him if he'd entertain at the next week's pie supper. The supper included a potluck, followed by music, recitations and a pie auction.

Emmett agreed. This was his big chance. He'd give his chalk-talk at the pie supper.

Four days before the performance, Emmett brushed off his Sunday black suit. He practiced tying his bow tie. He rubbed a cold biscuit on his leather shoes until they shone.

Emmett couldn't remember being so nervous. What if his hands shook so badly that he couldn't draw? What if he opened his mouth and no words came out? This was his first performance in front of an audience – actual human beings. He just hoped someone in the crowd was named either Charlie or Dan.

6

Good-Bye Farm

On Emmett's 18th birthday, December 9, 1916, he announced to his parents that he was moving to Houston, Missouri, to work in Dr. Haggard's drugstore.

Most of Emmett's friends had long since left the county and headed to St. Louis or Kansas City. They had factory jobs, most working on automobile assembly lines.

Emmett asked himself which one he should pick: the factory or the farm? He had to be honest with himself. He didn't want either. He knew his father hoped his son would stay on the farm, but Emmett wanted to work as a cartoonist. At least he wanted to try. If he failed, if he couldn't find work as an artist, then he'd pick one of them – the factory or the farm.

By January, Emmett was living in a Houston boardinghouse. During the day, he swept the floors at the drugstore, dusted the displays and restocked the shelves. At night, he practiced drawing. On Sunday evenings, he sat around the Freeland Hotel. He listened to the stories of traveling salesmen. These men were so clever and smart. Their work took them to cities all over the midwest. Three had been as far as Boston, Massachusetts. Emmett had never seen such men of the world.

In early spring, the salesmen were abuzz with talk of war. Pres. Woodrow Wilson asked the U.S. Congress to join the European Allies in a war against Germany. A week later, on April 6, the U.S. officially entered what would become known as World War I. The next month, Congress passed the Selective Service Act. It required all males from the ages of 21 to 30 to join the military service. Emmett was too young to join, but many men in town signed up or were drafted. Most local men went to boot camp in Waco, Texas. They sent home photographs of themselves in badly fitting uniforms.

24

Everybody seemed to have something important to do – either working in factories or preparing for war. Emmett was restless. All he did, day in, day out, was sweep out the drugstore. In his free time, he practiced his cartooning. But even cartooning seemed silly in the face of building cars and battling Germans. Emmett now had almost two dozen sketches that he kept in a large folder. And yet, what good did cartoons do anyone if they just sat in a folder?

Finally that winter, right after Emmett and his father hauled the last wagonload of corn to the train depot for shipment, Emmett made another announcement to his family. He was leaving Houston. Emmett reached in his pocket and pulled out a railroad ticket. It was a one-way ticket to Kansas City.

The ship on the right is the Lusitania. *When built, the British passenger liner was the largest and fastest ship in the world. On May 7, 1915, it was sunk off the coast of Ireland by a German U-boat. Of the 1,924 passengers and crew, 1,198 died — 144 were Americans. The sinking eventually helped bring the United States into World War I.*

7

The Big City

Emmett stared up at the vaulted ceiling of
Kansas City's Union Station. A long, tall corri-
dor stretched behind him, leading to the railroad
platforms. Emmett was sure that every building in
downtown Houston could fit into this one massive
station. Hundreds of people bustled around him.
Their voices echoed off the marble walls and floor.

For two hours Emmett wandered around Union
Station. He ate at the Fred Harvey restaurant. He
watched the endless flood of passengers coming
through that marble canyon. He listened to the
booming voice of the train announcer.

When he finally walked outside into the city, he
patted his pocket and felt the roll of dollar bills.
He'd saved almost $20 for this trip, enough to buy
his ticket and lodging for a few nights before he
found a job.

*Union Station,
Kansas City,
Missouri.*

Emmett picked out a boardinghouse a few blocks from the train station. The place looked cozy. There was a two-seater swing in the front yard. When Emmett knocked on the front door, a broad, cheerful woman answered. She told him a room, which he would share with another lodger, cost $5.00 a week and included all his meals.

Even though Emmett left home before sunrise, he didn't feel the least sleepy that first evening. After supper, he walked up and down the streets around the boardinghouse. The streets on this side of Union Station were lined with houses and small shops. Except for streetlights and a few front porch lights, the neighborhood seemed asleep.

Not so beyond Union Station. On the other side of the train tracks, downtown Kansas City lay in a lake of twinkling lights. The sky above the city glowed dark red from the lights of nightclubs and bars. The city's grand hotels and office buildings created a ragged outline against that sky.

Everything about this strange, new place thrilled him. Train smoke, streetcar bells, even the thick, sticky smell from the Wilson Meat Packing House – all of it filled his mind with a kind of breathless expectation. And he decided he would take it all in – the sights and sounds and smells – until it stopped being strange and new, until he became part of it.

The next day, Emmett rolled up his cartoon sketches, tucked them under his arm and headed downtown. Afraid of getting lost in the maze of busy streets, he climbed on a streetcar. The conductor let him off near the office of the *Kansas City Journal*.

Emmett stepped nervously inside the newspaper office. He asked the first person he saw if he could talk to someone about his cartoons. Emmett was

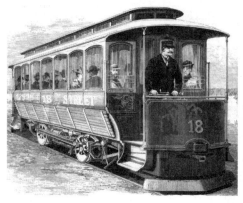

surprised to be led directly to the desk of the managing editor. The editor, leaning back in his swivel chair, flipped through the roll of drawings. He said he liked Emmett's work but that the *Journal* didn't have a job for a cartoonist.

Emmett tried his luck at the city's other newspaper, *The Kansas City Star*, which was much bigger than the *Journal*. But the *Star* editor showed no interest in the cartoons or in Emmett.

Emmett stepped back outside onto the busy streets of Kansas City. At a corner fruit stand, he bought a strange fruit, one that he'd never seen before. It looked like a giant orange, but it was yellow, like the apples on the farm. (It was a grapefruit, but Emmett didn't know that at the time.) He tried to eat the whole thing, skin and all. It was the bitterest, sourest thing he had ever tasted. He threw the torn pieces in the gutter in disgust. The taste in his mouth perfectly matched his mood.

"What difference did it make?" Emmett muttered to himself. Why be a cartoonist? That was just the dream of a country boy. Now he was a city boy. He would find a city job – and a city dream.

Job Jumping

That afternoon, Emmett set out to find a job – any job. The world wasn't going to come to an end just because he'd never be a cartoonist. It was unrealistic, he thought, to imagine that he – Emmett Kelly, the farm boy – could ever make his living as an artist.

He walked along the rail lines that ran through the industrial district. Dozens of warehouses and factories lined the route. He planned to ask at every company.

He got lucky on the second try. The Meridian Creamery Co. agreed to hire him, but he'd need to buy his

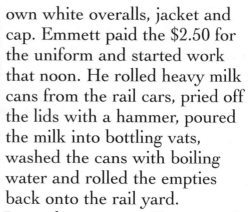

own white overalls, jacket and cap. Emmett paid the $2.50 for the uniform and started work that noon. He rolled heavy milk cans from the rail cars, pried off the lids with a hammer, poured the milk into bottling vats, washed the cans with boiling water and rolled the empties back onto the rail yard.

Later that summer, Emmett quit the creamery and hired on at a sign shop. He figured he knew a little about drawing, and the work wasn't as hard as rolling heavy milk cans. At the new job, Emmett worked with a man painting lettering on the side of the meat packing plant. They worked from a scaffold hung on the plant's wall near the roof. The painter liked to shake the scaffold and swing it from side to side. Emmett clutched the rope and tried not to look at the ground far below. The whole experience scared him so much that his hand shook until he could barely hold the paintbrush.

Through the slats in the scaffold Emmett could see the packing plant workers shoveling out the animal bones. At lunchtime, the workers sat on the dock to eat. Their aprons were covered in blood. The sight sickened Emmett until he couldn't eat.

Emmett quit the sign painting job and found work at the Columbia Steel Tank Co., painting the inside of tanks. The lead-based paint reeked in the close surroundings of the metal tank. Three days later, Emmett fainted from the fumes.

Next Emmett took a job at a lumberyard. He told the foreman that he could drive a truck – even though he could not. Emmett managed to steer the company's truck out of the driveway onto the city streets. Three blocks later, however, he created such a traffic jam that the police came.

By autumn, 1918, Emmett was starting to worry about jumping from job to job. In December, he would turn 21, the age for military service. Fortunately for Emmett, the war ended in November that year. By then Emmett was working at the Western Show Property Exchange. Owned by Doc Grubbs, an old medicine showman, the company produced cheap toys and souvenirs sold at carnivals and circuses. Emmett, along with several girls about Emmett's age, painted the bodies of plaster dolls. He earned six cents for each small doll and eight cents for big ones. The wages were good, but he also liked flirting with his co-workers.

With his money, Emmett bought a double-breasted jacket with a vest and a shirt with a starched collar. He bought gold-colored cuff links and wing-tip shoes. He bought tickets to vaudeville shows, moving picture shows and amusement parks. He saved some money, too. By Christmas he had $50 and train fare for home.

Emmett looked forward to going home for a visit. He hadn't been feeling well lately. It was probably all the late nights and exotic foods he'd been eating. He needed a break.

And besides, Emmett had a hundred big-city stories to tell his friends and family back on the farm. With steady work and a cozy place to live, he planned to do a little bragging. He was, after all, a sophisticated man of the city now, earning decent wages as…well, as an artist, of sorts.

9

Near Death

A parade of neighbors and old school friends dropped by the Kelly house to see Emmett his first night home. He still wasn't feeling well (he'd developed a little fever on the train trip) but he was glad to see everyone.

They seemed so impressed. He wore his fancy clothes and talked about all the important companies where he'd worked. Emmett liked to see their eyes widen with wonder when he boasted about his city life. He hinted broadly about the fine wages he made. He showed everyone postcards of Union Station, Electric Park, and other exciting places in Kansas City.

Sometimes, however, the visitors strayed from the subject of fancy clothes, important companies and exciting places. When Mrs. Clayton, his teacher, asked if he was still drawing cartoons,

Emmett talked about seeing Fatty Arbuckle and Charlie Chaplin at the Orpheum Theater. When Mr. Wheeler, a neighbor, asked if he was still doing his chalk-talk routine, Emmett talked about the pretty girls he knew.

The farm looked smaller than Emmett remembered. Years later he recalled his thoughts when he returned home that first time: "It was quiet and lonely and sort of dismal, too, I thought then. Within the short space of time I had spent in the big city, I had lost the farm forever."

Without anyone saying the words, Emmett's parents understood that he'd "lost the farm forever." But even so, Mr. Kelly put his arm around Emmett's shoulder. He said he was glad his son was finding his own way in the world.

The night before Emmett's trip back to Kansas City, his mother helped him pack. Strangely, she didn't talk much while they filled his cardboard suitcase. Finally, she picked up the gold-colored cuff links and stared at them for a moment. She held them out for Emmett to pack and said quietly that her and his father's dream was to own this farm. She hugged Emmett and told him that she hoped he'd find his dream, too.

In bed that night, Emmett thought about what she'd said. And it hurt his feelings. After all, hadn't he explained all about the fun of living in the big city? Didn't she see that he was now a man of the world? He was just like those salesmen he used to see at the Freeland Hotel in Houston. Country life was too quiet, he thought. Life in the city was exciting. Already he had had a half dozen jobs. Any night he could see a burlesque show or a movie. He could select a three-piece suit from more than a dozen clothing shops. He could walk the city streets from sunup to sundown and not see the same face twice.

Hope he'd find his dream! Why, hadn't he already found his dream?

The next morning, Emmett couldn't get out of bed. He raised his head and an ache shot through his shoulder muscles. In fact, every muscle in his body ached. His head felt as if it were clamped between a vice-grip. And he was so cold. He doubled up under the blankets, shivering until the mattress springs rattled. That was the last thing he remembered, until he heard his mother calling his name.

Emmett had influenza. His temperature was so high, for so long, that everyone thought he would die. That winter tens of thousands of people did die. Doc Haggard, like hundreds of other physicians, died of influenza while trying to help his sick patients. It was the pandemic of 1918. By the time it ended the next year, 15 million people worldwide had died of the viral illness. The number of dead in America was about 500,000 – more than died in World War I.

Even when Emmett was out of danger, he was still too weak to get out of bed. In his drowsy state,

he could hear his parents talking in the kitchen. They talked about trying a new strain of corn next spring. They talked about buying an additional 80 acres adjoining the farm. Listening to his mother and father reminded Emmett of those years back in Kansas. Even back then he heard them making plans for the future, plans to fulfill their dream.

Emmett remembered what his mother had said just before he was sick. She hoped he'd find his dream. What was his dream? As a little boy, he'd dreamed of being a musician, a railroad worker and a carnival daredevil. Not too long ago, he'd told himself that his dream was to be an artist. Sure, he painted kewpie dolls at Dr. Grubbs' carnival supply company, but Emmett knew that didn't make him an artist. He'd gone to Kansas City to find work as a cartoonist. That hadn't worked out.

So what? He had a job. He had friends. He had money. He had fun. What more could a fellow want, he thought. So he wouldn't be an artist. Again, so what? Life wouldn't end just because he wouldn't be an artist.

But life could end, couldn't it? In an instant, it seemed to Emmett, he had gone from being well to being sick, near death. Life could have ended, and he never would have been an artist. Never would have been anything.

Emmett rolled over and looked out the window and across the field. He could see the pond in the distance. He remembered the morning that the cloud hovered over it, threatening to end his hopes of going to the Old Settlers Reunion. That was the trouble with dreams; there were so many things that could go wrong. Dreams sometimes didn't work out.

And there was something particularly trouble-some about Emmett's dream. He'd hoped to be an

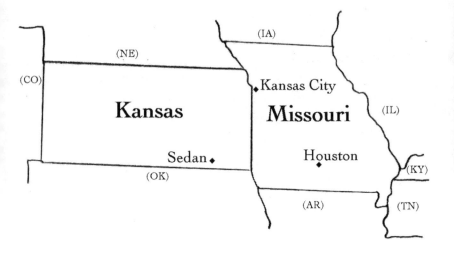

artist, and he was sure he had the skill, but he wasn't really sure what kind of artist he wanted to be. A cartoonist? A sign painter? A chalk-talk artist? A scene painter for circuses?

No, dreams didn't always work out. But one thing was sure: Emmett had never given his dream a chance.

He heard a knock at the door. His mother came in and set a lunch tray on his bedside table.

Emmett turned to see her smiling face. "I'm going to be an artist," he said.

And in a way he wouldn't have suspected, he would keep that promise.

🎏10🎏

Sad Little Man

Emmett stood on the viaduct and looked down at the train tracks. Dozens of tracks, like endless black ribbons, stretched out behind Union Station. On one of those tracks were 100 railcars belonging to the Ringling Brothers and Barnum & Bailey Circus.

Four weeks ago, he'd gone to the John Robinson's Circus. It was the biggest show Emmett had ever seen. The man seated next to Emmett noticed his look of amazement, and he told Emmett that Robinson was small compared to some circuses.

"And none of them," the man added, "compares with The Big One."

Emmett hadn't heard of "The Big One."

"That's what it's called – Ringling Brothers and

41

The Ringling brothers lived in Baraboo, Wisconsin. They started their first circus in 1884. The show started with nine wagons and used local farm workers to move their equipment. This very old photograph shows ticket takers at the Ringling circus.

Barnum & Bailey Circus," said the man. "It needs a hundred train cars to travel."

Emmett didn't believe the man. He knew trains, and he knew that 100 train cars stretched almost a mile. Four weeks later, however, Emmett discovered that the man was telling the truth.

Early one morning, the Ringling circus arrived in Kansas City. Watching from the viaduct over the tracks, Emmett counted each of the 100 rail cars — and these weren't the usual 40-foot cars. The circus cars were 60 or 70 feet long. That made the circus train well over a mile. (Railroads charged customers for each car they used. To get the most for their money, some circuses built extra long cars.)

Emmett didn't have the 75 cents for a Ringling ticket, but he saw the back lot of the circus. It was like a little town. It had a blacksmith shop, cooking and dining tents, a barbershop, an electric power generator, water wagons and a man who delivered mail every day.

Ever since he saw Robinson and Ringling, Emmett couldn't stop thinking about circuses. One day, while rummaging around in the back room of Doc Gruggs' Western Show Property Exchange, he'd found the bar and crane for a trapeze. The rig lacked all its ropes, but Emmett bought it anyway and stuffed the box under his bed. He couldn't explain what made him buy it. What could he ever do with a trapeze, for heavens sake? After all, he nearly got sick from working on scaffolding.

After he saw the Robinson circus, Emmett asked the show's manager for a job. He thought he might find work as a wagon or scene painter. No luck. But Emmett was too dazzled by the gigantic Ringling circus to ask for a job there.

When Emmett returned to Kansas City from Houston, Doc Grubbs sent him on a job for the Zieger's United Shows. Emmett took the Zieger job because he believed it might lead him closer to becoming a full-time artist. Circuses used paintings and cartoons. To advertise upcoming shows, they

One of the most exciting times of the year for most American towns was the day the traveling circus arrived. Even when shows were sold out or the tickets were expensive, children sometimes found unofficial ways to see the circus, as this 1915 photograph shows.

created beautifully drawn posters and billboards. Circus wagons were painted with wonderful, dramatic circus scenes.

The Zieger show was in winter quarters in Weston, Missouri. Emmett painted the merry-go-round. He earned $20 a week. The word "United" in the carnival's name made it sound grand, but it was anything but grand. The entire operation, tents, rides and the three sideshows, fit into two small train cars. One morning Emmett woke up scratching, and he discovered that he was infested with lice. That's when Emmett decided to quit.

Back in Kansas City, Emmett found a job at the Adagram Film Company. The company created advertisement films shown at silent movie theaters. For each ad, Emmett drew a figure and then created several poses for the same figure. A photographer filmed each pose. When shown on the screen, the final film made the string of poses look like a moving image of the original figure.

Emmett often went to the movie theater where he could see his little black-ink drawings turned into motion-picture cartoons. Emmett later remembered, "Whenever the audience laughed at one of my cartoons, I'd be proud as a movie star at the premiere of his own picture."

One day Mr. Whitcomb, Emmett's boss, needed an ad for a local bakery. Emmett sat down at the drawing board and began to sketch the face of a man. A sad little man. A hobo with a potbelly and baggy pants. Emmett drew him in dozens of poses – running, walking, standing on his head, but whatever the pose, the little man's face stayed the same – sad and lonely.

Emmett might have gone on drawing cartoons at Adagram. He was happy doing the work. But a year later, in 1921, he had the chance to travel with a circus. He wanted work as a painter, but the circus manager wasn't hiring painters. And so Emmett suddenly announced that he could also do trapeze work.

What made him say such a thing? He would never know. But his face must not have betrayed the simple fact that heights made him squeamish because, to Emmett's surprise, the manager hired him. Even more surprising, Emmett quickly taught himself the basics of trapeze.

And he might have gone on being a minor act on the trapeze, which he was for the next few years. He was happy doing that work, too. But a strange thing happened. A sad little man – once made of black ink and born on a drawing board in Kansas City – stepped off the page. His name was Weary Willie, and he became the world's most famous clown.

❧ 11 ❧

The Grift Show

The parade was beginning. A long line of circus performers sat mounted on 100 horses. They waited outside the tent for the music to start. Emmett was one of the performers. He felt a little uneasy. His mount was the tallest horse he'd ever seen – except for the other 99 amazingly tall horses in the Howe's Great London Circus.

Started before the Civil War, Howe's was one of the oldest traveling shows in the country. Many of its performers had been with the circus for several years. That was why Emmett hated to seem like such a rookie. He sat up tall in the saddle, trying to look like an experienced horseman.

This was the show's opening parade – the Garland Entry – and every performer rode in it. A circus was a community. "Everybody pitches in," Dan Odum, the circus manager said, when Emmett

47

During the 1850s American circuses began using a parade as a way to announce their arrival in town. This tradition eventually developed into a giant pageant of colorful wagons and exotic animals. The tradition of the circus parade lasted for more than 75 years.

showed up for work in Lancaster, Missouri, the winter quarters of the circus.

That first day, Emmett and the other performers loaded the horses, camels, seven elephants and freshly painted wagons into 25 railroad cars. In those years, performers also did double duty during the show. Besides performing on the trapeze, Emmett also worked as one of the 12 whiteface clowns.

The music suddenly began. In single file, the long parade of horses and riders pranced into the tent.

Emmett knew the routine perfectly. The performers rode around the ring in front of the audience. Each rider carried a 10-foot long stick thickly covered in roses and lilies. Weighted with the flowers, Emmett's stick drooped in a long, heavy arch.

Finally the riders formed a giant circle. After two blasts from the announcer's whistle, the riders trotted forward, creating two parallel rows. The rows then spun off into two circles. It was an impressive sight – 100 horses and riders prancing together in a flowery display. At least it was impressive when – and if – it worked.

The first problem, however, was that Emmett wasn't a good rider. On the farm, he rode Charlie, the family's work horse. But Charlie was short and dumpy and had the energy of a sleeping turtle. Luckily, Frank Miller, Howe's equestrian director, had given Emmett an elderly and gentle horse.

The second problem was the stick. It bounced and bobbed around like a June bug. Emmett could hardly hold onto the horse and the garland at the same time. As the line of riders made their first circle, Emmett's long stick whipped this way and that. He tried to hold it steady, but the end of the garland flipped back and hit the rider trotting behind Emmett. It then shot around and slapped

Emmett's horse in the face. The horse jumped and the saddle, which hadn't been secured properly, slid sideways. Emmett toppled to the ground.

But Emmett was quick. He caught the horse and remounted. For the rest of the parade, he rode bareback.

The roustabouts (temporary workers) shown here are putting up The Big Top, the circus' main tent. Raising tents was a major part of getting a show ready. The Big Top for large circuses was often 500 feet long and 200 feet wide. [A football field is 360 feet long and 160 feet wide.] The tent was raised in every town where the circus appeared. A season, which ran from spring to late fall, might include shows in 140 towns, with 120 of those a single day each.

Frank Miller was impressed. Surely, only an expert horseman could recover his horse so smoothly. From then on Miller gave Emmett only young and spirited horses to ride.

Many things happened on Emmett's first circus tour. In Hastings, Nebraska, the show hit a windstorm. The "blowdown" tore up the cookhouse tent, sideshow, and padroom (dressing room). A rainstorm followed. Later in Devil's Lake, North Dakota, a swarm of mosquitoes invaded. The insects attacked everything, including the horses who bucked the riders and then stampeded. At daybreak one morning, three of the circus's train cars derailed. The only serious damage was to the cook's car. The 100-pound bags of flour burst. Emmett later said it looked like a snowstorm.

None of this dampened Emmett's enthusiasm. Circus people were troupers. That meant they performed no matter what happened. "The show must go on," Dan Odum said after each disaster. Wind, rain, bugs, wreck – the troupers rebuilt, dried out, dusted off and went on with the performance.

By the end of the season, the Howe's Circus had traveled 18,365 miles. The big shows, like Ringling Bros. and Barnum & Bailey Circus, started on the east coast. Howe's wanted to avoid that competition. So they opened in New Mexico, traveled through the western states and into Canada. Then they toured the midwest and worked their way south. They finally ended in Florida.

Emmett was glad it was over. He was a trouper, but one thing bothered him. Howe's was a grift show. Gamblers traveled with the circus. In the sideshow, they cheated at cards or played sleight-of-hand tricks on unsuspecting customers. This often caused serious trouble for the rest of the troupers. Frequently, the circus had to pack up and leave in a hurry. After one show, several angry townsmen, who'd been cheated, chased the circus train as it pulled out of the depot. Emmett had gone to town and didn't know the circus was leaving. He had to jump aboard as the train sped away from the mob.

After the final performance in Florida, Emmett picked up his paycheck and started to leave. Dan Odum stopped him. He told Emmett he was going with the John Robinson's Circus next spring. Emmett remembered seeing that wonderful show in Kansas City.

"Would you like to join the outfit?" Odum asked.

❧ 12 ❧

Death and Birth

Emmett's father sat in a wheelchair on the train station platform at Houston, Missouri. A few weeks earlier, Mr. Kelly had a stroke, a blocked blood vessel to the brain. The family sent a telegram to Emmett.

After the Howe's tour, Emmett found winter work with the St. Louis Police Circus. Before he could join the Robinson circus the following spring, he received the news about his father. Emmett returned home at once. "I'll never forget my dad's face when I put my arms around him," he said later.

Though Mr. Kelly could barely move his body, his eyes followed Emmett's every move. Emmett was arguing with the station's officials. He was angry. The railroad company refused to allow Mr. Kelly aboard the train. He was sick, the officials said, and sick people couldn't ride with the other passengers.

Emmett's sister, Sylvia, was now married and lived in Mulberry Grove, Illinois. After Mr. Kelly's stroke, the Kellys sold their Missouri farm and planned to move to a farm near Sylvia in Illinois.

"He's not contagious," Emmett told the station officials. "Nobody's going to catch any disease from him."

But the officials were firm. Mr. Kelly couldn't ride in the passenger compartment. If Emmett agreed, however, to sign a form that stated his father didn't have a disease, Mr. Kelly could travel in the baggage car. Emmett didn't want his father to endure any more public embarrassment, and so he signed the form.

Two years working the trapeze had greatly strengthened Emmett's upper-body muscles. He had no trouble lifting his father into the train and placing him on a cot in the corner of the baggage car. Emmett stayed with Mr. Kelly all the way to Illinois.

After settling his parents on their new farm, Emmett headed off to join the John Robinson Circus. The show featured dozens of acts — all sorts of animal acts, acrobats, jugglers, Wild West stars, equestrian riders, high-wire and trapeze acts.

One of the trapeze acts was the Moore family. Mr. Moore had trained his five daughters and two sons since they were toddlers. Emmett liked to see them work. He especially enjoyed watching one of the daughters: Eva Moore. On some evenings, Emmett and Eva sat on the wardrobe trunks in the back lot and stared at the moon. They pretended that the circus band was serenading them when it played the popular song, "The Same Silvery Moon."

Emmett and Eva fell in love. Mr. Moore, however, didn't like the two young people seeing each other. He was afraid the Moore trapeze act would break up if the two married. Even so, Emmett and Eva eloped one afternoon when the circus was in Charlottesville, Virginia.

As it turned out, Mr. Moore didn't lose a daughter. He gained another trapeze performer.

Emmett and Eva teamed up and formed "The Aerial Kellys," a double trapeze act. The two spent many hours practicing new tricks on the trapeze. Emmett taught himself to hang by his teeth, a routine called the "iron-jaw" act. Emmett built the rigging. He found a hard piece of rubber, big enough to fit in his mouth. He attached a swivel to it and then fastened a strap to the swivel. With the "iron-jaw" rig in his mouth, Emmett hung by his legs from the trapeze, while Eva swung from a bar that was fastened to the strap.

Being an aerialist wasn't what Emmett had in mind when he dreamed of working as an artist. But practicing new trapeze tricks made him feel just as creative as when he used to do his chalk talk routine.

One day Odum saw Emmett sketching new costume ideas for "The Aerial Kellys." The manager liked the work and hired Emmett to draw a picture of the circus's major performers. The circus used the picture in a newspaper advertisement in Canada.

Emmett was glad for the extra work and wages because he and Eva were going to have a baby. In preparation for their growing family, he started saving money – pinching pennies, as Eva liked to tease him.

Emmett felt good about his circus career – except his work as a whiteface clown. Robinson Circus had almost two dozen clowns, and they all worked in whiteface. That was a circus tradition. Circus performers came from all over the world – Europe, Asia and Africa. Circus communities were a rich mix of cultures and colors. Each circus performer worked hard to create a fabulous, one-of-a-kind act. And yet every clown had to be alike. They all covered their faces, necks and hands with a mixture of zinc oxide and lard – the makeup of the whiteface.

One day Emmett was rummaging around in his trunk and found a drawing from his time at Adagram in Kansas City. It was the sad-face hobo. The next morning he went to a second hand store and bought a pair of baggy pants and an old shirt. He also found a beat-up hat and scuffed shoes. That night, at the evening show, Emmett dressed in his hobo costume.

After the performance, Kenneth Waite, the head clown, found Emmett. He said he didn't want the clowns looking like tramps. "People don't like to see a dirty clown," he said. "You'll wear whiteface, just like the rest of us."

Emmett couldn't explain why Waite's dislike of the hobo clown upset him. But it did. Emmett went to Odum and complained. "The clown boss has the final word," said Odum.

Emmett could feel his neck turning red. He hadn't been this mad since the railroad officials made his father ride in the baggage car. Why did he feel like this? After all, clowning wasn't Emmett's real job. It wasn't what he really cared about. He'd be perfectly satisfied trapezing and drawing circus ads for the rest of his life. But in that moment, an angry Emmett came very close to quitting the Robinson Circus.

Lose his job over a sad, little hobo? No. He had responsibilities. He was about to be a father.

Not long afterwards, while the circus was in Canada, Emmett received a telegram. His father was dead.

Sometimes it was good to dress up as a clown – even a whiteface clown. A person could hide behind that zinc oxide and lard. Emmett could hide his sadness, which he did until the last day of the circus season.

On that day, November 24, 1924, joy replaced sadness. Emmett Kelly, Jr. was born.

❧ 13 ❧

From Ragtag To Robinson

The next spring, Emmett and Eva bought a Ford roadster and headed south. They were looking for any circus work they could find. The John Robinson Circus had renewed the Aerial Kellys' contract, but Emmett said no. The circus didn't allow babies to travel with the show. Although Emmett's mother offered to take Emmett Jr. during the 40-week circus season, Emmett and Eva couldn't part with him.

In a little town in Tennessee, Emmett noticed a poster advertising the Mighty Haag Show. It was the first circus Emmett ever saw, back in Missouri when he was 17 years old.

Emmett and Eva set out to find The Hog Show, as circus people called it. They tracked the show for three days. Each day the roads became rougher and rougher. Finally they spotted the circus near a tiny hamlet in the hills. Luckily, the show's double-trapeze act had recently left, and the Aerial Kellys landed a job. It didn't pay well, but at least it was work.

Compared to the Robinson Circus, the Haag circus was small and ragtag. It was a truck show, not prosperous enough to travel by train. The main tent was so little that when Emmett hung from the trapeze, he almost touched the ground. Its ceiling was much too low to do the "iron jaw" routine. Sometimes the circus stopped at a crossroads, not a building in sight. But by evening, Emmett looked outside the tent and saw the lights of hundreds of lanterns, carried by the hill people, coming toward the circus.

Mr. Haag, the circus owner, gave away tickets to local storeowners in exchange for feed for the circus animals and other supplies. One day the circus parked next to a turkey farm. At night the birds perched on the sleeping tent. The next day Emmett noticed that the birds had disappeared. For many days afterwards, the cook served turkey dinners.

The Haag circus wasn't a safe place to raise a child. Sometimes members of the audience became rowdy. Fistfights broke out. Occasionally someone in the audience pulled out a gun and shot holes through the tent roof.

Emmett and Eva barely made enough money to live. At the end of that season, they only had $40. Emmett had to mortgage the roadster for extra money.

Emmett knew that next year he and Eva would have to find another circus. Back in Mulberry Grove at his mother's farm, Emmett contacted Dan Odum. Soon afterwards, Emmett received a letter from the Robinson circus manager. It said that the circus didn't need a double trapeze act, the kind that the Aerial Kellys offered. If Emmett wanted a job, he would have to do a single act and double as a whiteface clown. There was nothing for Eva except work on the ladder, an aerial act similar to the chorus line in theater.

Eva wanted to work on the trapeze, but the couple's only other offer paid much less than Robinson. And worse, the other show was another ragtag circus. Emmett didn't want to do whiteface. He remembered the disagreement with Waite. And yet, except for powerful Ringling Bros., the Robinson show was the biggest circus in the country.

In the end, Emmett swallowed his pride. He and Eva left Emmett Jr. with Mrs. Kelly and signed on with Robinson again.

King Bros. Circus performers are shown here in the late 19ᵗʰ century. The circus played small towns but was one of the oldest and longest lasting circuses in American history. Note the whiteface clown seated in the center.

14

Finding Courage

Emmett stared down at the woman. Blood covered her legs and head. She was Mabel Stark, the tiger trainer. Moments earlier, two of her giant cats attacked her during the wild animal performance.

One cat tore open Stark's left thigh. The gash ripped through to the bone. The second cat then leaped from his pedestal and grabbed Stark's right leg. Stark fell, and just as she hit the ground, the first cat's paw struck the side of the trainer's head. Part of her scalp was torn away.

Emmett's trapeze act was scheduled right after Stark's big cat act. He'd been standing outside the big tent when he heard the screams. Emmett had never seen so much blood.

Emmett and two other circus employees carried Stark's torn body to a truck. Behind him, Emmett could hear the horrified screams of the audience. Stark was the first woman to train and perform with wild animals in a circus, and she was a favorite of the audience. A former nurse, Stark fell in love with the big cats when, as a young woman, she saw them at a circus.

Almost from the first day, the 1928 season had been one disaster after another. Spring rains washed out opening day in West Baden, Indiana. The tent sagged when the giant poles that held up the canvas shifted under the swampy ground.

The rains continued. In Canada, it rained for 21 days. All the tents were soaked. Later during the

Mabel Stark is shown here with three of her cats, a jaguar and two Bengal tigers.

tour, two giraffes died. No one knew for sure why. Now the show was in Bangor, Maine, where Mabel Stark was mauled in one of the worst cat attacks in circus history.

For Emmett, things weren't any better on a personal level. During the season, Eva complained bitterly about doing the ladder act. She missed the trapeze, which she'd trained for all of her life. Emmett understood her frustration. He agreed to talk to Odum about letting them work again as the Aerial Kellys. A few days later, Odum finally agreed to the double trapeze act.

Maybe their luck was changing, Emmett thought.

He began immediately to work on new routines for the double act. Eva was excited to be on the trapeze again. When the 1929 season started, the future looked bright for the Kellys.

But the future wasn't bright. The disasters were just beginning – not just for Eva and Emmett, but for the entire country.

In October, just before the end of the circus season, John Ringling, owner of the Ringling show, bought the John Robinson Circus and several other shows.

Now Ringling was the king of the circus world. He owned all the big shows. But his triumph was brief. Within a few days of Ringling's big purchases, New York City's Wall Street stock market crashed. The worst financial depression in the nation's history had begun.

It would also be the worst time in circus history. Performers lost jobs. Circuses closed. The first to close was the 125-year-old John Robinson Circus. America's oldest circus folded before the end of the 1930 season, and it would never open again.

The Aerial Kellys' future was uncertain. After Robinson closed, Emmett and Eva performed double trapeze with the Sells-Floto Circus, but it, too, closed within a year. In 1933, the Hagenbeck-Wallace Circus offered Emmett a full time clowning job – no aerial work.

Eva was an excellent aerialist, and she didn't want Emmett to accept a clowning contract. But he was afraid they might not find any work if he didn't take the clown job. The two quarreled more and more. Emmett told Eva that he knew about poverty and was saving against it. Eva was pregnant with their second child, and Emmett felt the couple needed to make as much money as possible. As each month passed during the Depression, tens of thousands of Americans lost their jobs. Any day, Emmett might lose his job, too. But Eva was tired of the scrimping and saving. Eva said that after the baby was born, she would only return to the circus if she could work as a principal aerialist.

Shortly before the 1934 circus season began, Emmett's second son, Patrick Thomas, was born. Emmett barely had the chance to see the new baby before leaving for the tour. True to her word, Eva didn't return to the circus with Emmett. There was no aerial work.

Emmett sent money home to Eva and the boys, but he knew that his marriage was in trouble. A few months later, he received a packet of papers. Eva had filed for divorce. The marriage was over.

These were hard times. It wasn't that Emmett wanted to be a whiteface clown. He didn't. He realized that many of the whiteface clowns were extraordinarily talented. They made Emmett laugh. He'd learned much about clowning from them and many would remain his lifelong friends.

But for Emmett, whiteface clowning was just a job. Sometimes he merely went through the motions of clowning – standing on his head, turning somersaults, jumping on the backs of other whiteface clowns. The white fluffy wig and ruffled collar, the feverish, nonstop routines – it was all silliness.

That night during the performance, after receiving the divorce papers, Emmett thought about Mabel Stark. Stark only weighed 100 pounds. Her cats weighed 600 pounds. Stark liked to say that her work didn't take strength. Every time she stepped into the big cage, she matched wits with the tigers. That didn't take strength. It took skill and courage. For a brief moment in Bangor, Maine, her skill failed her but not her courage.

At the hospital Stark had directed the doctors to pour carbolic acid into the deep wounds in her legs. The immediate danger, Stark knew, was infection. The doctors sewed up the gashes and bandaged the wounds. They didn't believe she would live. But she did. Stark later said that if she died her cats would have been called murderers and either spent their lives in tiny cages or been killed. "That thought," she later said, "gave me strength to fight." A few weeks later, still in bandages and using a cane, Stark stepped once again into the big cage under the big top. Like the thousands of people who watched that night, Emmett applauded until his hands ached.

The divorce weighed heavily on Emmett's heart. He had to find the courage to keep going. He'd never felt so sad. Suddenly he thought about the sad-face hobo, the one he'd drawn in Kansas City.

Right then Emmett decided he wouldn't do whiteface any more. He couldn't do the silliness. Not any more. It would take courage, but somehow he'd convince the circus manager to let him do a different clown – a hobo clown. "Maybe the audience won't like him," Emmett would say. "But just let me try."

But the audience *did* like the hobo clown. And Emmett never returned to whiteface – except a few years later, when he murdered someone.

❧ 15 ❧

The Hobo Arrives

The clown stared into the empty peanut bag. Lifting his head to the audience, the clown looked mournfully up at the faces in the crowd. The people in the bleachers watched him. They'd never seen a clown like this one.

The parade was over, and as usual, a swarm of clowns came running and jumping into the arena. They entertained the audience while the animal trainers, aerialists and other performers set up their rigs. All the clowns were whiteface – except this one.

This one was a hobo, dressed in ragged clothes and an old brown derby hat. He had a sad face and walked slowly, like a man carrying a heavy weight on his shoulders. So sad was the face that the audience didn't know whether to laugh at him or feel sorry for him. Slowly the clown strolled over to a row of people. He stared longingly at their full bags of peanuts and candy. His sad eyes watched people eat. He peered again into his empty bag. Shrugging his shoulders wearily, he turned to walk away.

A little boy, sitting beside his parents, leaned over the railing and offered a peanut to the clown. At first the clown looked surprised. The sad clown never spoke, but his expression seemed to say, "For me?" With shy gratitude, the clown took the peanut from the boy. It was just a small gift, but the hobo stared at it as if it were a treasured jewel.

The clown then placed the peanut between his teeth and tried to bite down on it. The peanut wouldn't crack. The clown tried harder. Still the peanut didn't break.

By now every one on that side of the circus tent stared at the sad-face clown with the peanut. The clown walked to a nearby tent pole. After picking up a 16-pound sledgehammer propped against the pole, he returned to the little boy.

It took a few circus seasons before Emmett found just the right clothes and make up for his sad-face clown. This was the first. Page 71 shows a later variation.

The sad-face clown brushed off an empty bleacher seat and gently set the peanut on the seat. He carefully raised the sledgehammer above the tiny peanut.

The audience, guessing what was going to happen next, began to giggle.

The clown dropped the hammer. It made a heavy thud. Believing he had finally cracked the peanut, the hobo raised the hammer and peered underneath.

To his dismay, the peanut was little more than a brown smudge. Nothing was left of the nut and shell.

Looking sadder than ever, the poor clown strolled away across the sawdust floor, leaving the laughing audience behind him.

One night, in New Haven, Connecticut, Emmett found an elegantly dressed man standing by his costume trunk in clown alley. The man introduced himself as Bernard Mills.

Emmett knew the name. Everyone knew the name. The man's family owned the famous British show: Bertram Mills London Olympia Circus. Emmett knew that the British circus was in the U.S. to find acts for its six-week winter season.

"May I speak with you, Mr. Kelly?" Mr. Mills asked. Elegantly dressed in a pin-striped suit, Mills pronounced each word in his precise, clipped British accent.

Still wearing his hobo costume, Emmett nodded. He felt like a dandelion next to an orchid.

Mr. Mills asked if Emmett was interested in working as a clown in the Mills show. In addition to a salary, the circus would pay for Emmett's passage to England.

Emmett, who certainly wanted the job, surprised himself by coolly asking how much money the job paid. He was professional, he told himself. He shouldn't rush into things.

The salary Mills offered was good – better than Emmett could earn doing other winter work – and the opportunity to travel overseas thrilled Emmett.

And yet, Emmett worried that the British wouldn't understand his American hobo routines. Emmett had heard that American and British audiences were very different. People in Great Britain dressed up for the circus. Many wore evening clothes – fancy gowns and stiff, white shirts, monocles and opera glasses. British politicians and royalty attended the circus. Emmett knew he could make American audiences laugh. With his peanut routine and others like it, he'd made them laugh for five years. They called the hobo clown Weary Willie, a name given to him by a newspaper reporter. Americans understood the quirky, sad antics of Emmett's hobo. But would the fancy-dressed British find a hobo funny?

Willie Weary performed many clown routines. One of the most popular was the one shown here, smashing the peanut.

16

Escaping War

Emmett spotted the castle when he stepped from the train. Its ivy-covered tower was like something in a fairy tale.

This was his second winter job with the Mills circus. The show was traveling through Kent in the country's southeast. Since his first performance in England a year earlier, Emmett's fears about British reaction to Weary Willie were relieved. He was as popular with British audiences as he was with American.

At the top of the castle, Emmett walked along the battlements. He'd seen Hollywood war movies set in medieval

times – ancient knights wearing swords and chain mail armor and using battering rams to attack castles similar to this one.

Emmett was thinking about this when he suddenly saw something that made him feel uneasy. It was an air-raid siren. Its new metal casing looked out of place on this ancient tower. But Emmett knew that it wasn't out of place. It was part of Britain's ARP (Air Raid Precautions). From the circus train, he'd seen British artillery practicing and troops drilling in the countryside.

It was 1939, and signs of war were everywhere. In Germany, Adolf Hitler had taken over Austria and part of Czechoslovakia. When he threatened to move into other countries, Britain and France agreed to stop the German expansion.

Emmett was nervous about the talk of war. He wanted to leave for home *before* war broke out between England and Germany. Other non-British circus performers, who had been in England during World War I, said that leaving the country after the war started was almost impossible. Consequently, Emmett agreed to perform for the Mills circus only with the understanding that if war seemed about to happen he could leave for the U.S. – even in the middle of the season.

On September 1, 1939, the circus played in Brighton, a port town south of London. Brighton was a popular holiday spot, and everyone was in a festive mood. The opening act had just begun when

Bernard Mills interrupted the performance. A hush fell over the audience. Emmett felt the hairs on his neck stand up.

The microphone crackled and Mills announced, "At five o'clock this morning, Germany invaded Poland. Warsaw has been bombed. Thousands are feared dead."

The show continued, but many people in the audience left soon after the announcement. Few people came to the evening performance. All over the country people sat listening to their radios. The British government had pledged to come to Poland's aid if the Germans attacked. War might come any moment.

After the show, Emmett walked along the harbor to the office of the U.S. Steamship Lines. He asked the office clerk for a ticket on the next ship to America.

The clerk shook his head. "Booked solid," he said. "We've even added 300 cots, and they're all taken." He said the next American passenger ship, the *Manhattan*, would leave in two days. "But I can't guarantee it'll make it to New York. If war breaks out, it'll turn back for Brighton."

Emmett took his chances and bought a ticket on the *Manhattan*.

Two days later, a huge crowd gathered on the dock. Emmett made his way through the mob of people pleading with *Manhattan* officials to let them aboard. "I'll sleep on the deck," one man called out.

But the ship was already booked beyond capacity. Hundreds of cots, set up for the overflow, filled the hallways and public rooms of the *Manhattan*.

When the ship finally headed to sea, Emmett stood on deck, sadly watching all the people left behind.

The morning after leaving port, the *Manhattan* received a news cable. At 11:30 a.m., the ship's steward announced to the passengers, "Thirty minutes ago, the British government declared war on Germany."

And so it began. World War II was the deadliest conflict in human history. It involved dozens of nations around the world. By the time the war ended in 1945, almost 20 million soldiers and many more civilians died. The dead included one million Americans.

Not long after the first news cable, a second one reached the *Manhattan*: a German submarine had just sunk a British passenger liner departing from Greenock, Scotland, a port near the *Manhattan's* shipping lane.

The *Manhattan* was now in danger. Trying to avoid a German attack, the *Manhattan's* captain raised an American flag, to show the Germans that the ship was from the U.S., a neutral nation in the war. Even at night two spotlights shone on the flag.

As Emmett strolled around the ship one day, he saw a sheet of canvas covering a small boat. Several Englishmen stood guard around it. Emmett recognized the covered object: a PT boat, a fast craft used to torpedo enemy ships. He soon learned that the boat was being shipped to America as a model for mass production in the U.S. factories. This was very dangerous. Germany wouldn't hesitate to bomb any passenger ship that carried military equipment.

I am telling you

On June 28th I expect you to enlist in the army of war savers to back up my army of fighters.
W. S. S. Enlistment

On December 7, 1941, the Japanese military bombed Pearl Harbor, the U.S. naval base in Hawaii. The next morning Emmett went to the naval recruiting office to sign up for the military. Like thousands of other men and women, Emmett's first thought after hearing of the attack was to volunteer to serve the country. The day after the bombing, the U.S. Congress declared war on Japan. Before long, America would join Great Britain and its allies in World War II. The military did not accept 42-year-old Emmett, but it did take his 18-year-old son, Emmett Jr.

U.S. WAR BONDS

When the *Manhattan* approached Newfoundland one night, Emmett and the other passengers noticed hundreds of lights in the water. The captain explained that the lights were fishing boats. He'd steered the ship close to the small boats so that the fishermen could come to the rescue if a German submarine attacked the *Manhattan*.

Tension was high on the ship. Everyone expected that the next moment would bring disaster. Passengers stared out at the ocean and imagined they saw the telescope of a German submarine. Some thought they saw the bubbling trail of an approaching torpedo.

There were many children onboard. To relieve the children's fear, a group of passengers organized a stage show. They asked Emmett to perform. *Manhattan's* crew dug deep inside the ship's baggage area to find Emmett's circus trunk with the clown makeup and hobo costume. Emmett later wrote that on the day of the show, people momentarily forgot the terrible threat of a submarine attack. Willie Weary became a Pied Piper. Laughing children followed him wherever he went.

Several days later, in the early morning, Emmett walked out on the deck. Off in the distance he saw a sight he never forgot. Years later, tears would well in his eyes whenever he described the moment. "I have seen some beautiful women…," he wrote, "but nothing to touch the Lady who met us in the New York harbor. It made my eyes fill with tears to see her standing there, the torch of liberty lifted in her hand."

❄ 17 ❄

The Clown and the Artist

Emmett didn't have a job when the *Manhattan* landed in New York. During his last winter in London, he'd met John Ringling North, the owner of the Ringling Bros. & Barnum Bailey Circus. Emmett hoped that Ringling might offer the hobo clown a job. No such luck.

For the next year, Emmett worked in nightclubs doing his chalk-talk act. He even had a small role in a Broadway musical. But the play received poor reviews and closed within a few weeks. Then in late 1941, Emmett found a thick envelope in his mailbox. It was a contract and a letter from Pat Valdo, the head of performers for the Ringling

circus. Would Emmett come to work for the circus?

The Big One. Big Bertha. The Ringling circus had many nicknames. Mostly it was known as "The Greatest Show on Earth." This was the biggest opportunity of Emmett's career.

✛

The circus began its 1942 season in Madison Square Garden, New York City. For longer than anyone could remember, the circus had opened in "The Garden." Emmett felt like a starry-eyed kid when he arrived for work the first day. The most famous circus performers in the world worked for Ringling. Everywhere Emmett looked were circus stars.

When the wardrobe boss spotted Emmett, he told him to go down to the dressing room and try on his costumes. Emmett was confused. He only had one costume – his hobo outfit. The wardrobe boss explained that Emmett was scheduled to perform in several skits, and each skit required a different costume.

Emmett didn't know what to do. Here was his big opportunity – to work for the world's most famous circus. How could he tell them that he couldn't wear strange costumes? He was *only* the sad-face clown. Weary Willie wasn't like other clowns. For people in the audience to understand

Willie, they had to watch the hobo's performance over the course of two or three skits. Emmett remembered the first time American and British audiences saw Willie. They didn't know whether to laugh or feel sorry for the strange clown. Getting to know Willie took time. Willie wasn't a big splashy character. He didn't run around, crash into things, make loud noises. Willie moved slowly. His actions were small and quiet. If Emmett made several costume changes during a show, how could the audience get to know Willie?

Ringling Circus was the Greatest Show on Earth. They had dozens of clowns. Emmett was just one. If he complained, he was taking a big chance. John Murray Anderson, the production manager, would surely fire him.

Emmett found Anderson inside the auditorium, taking care of last minute details for tomorrow's dress rehearsal. Emmett said that he didn't want to upset any plans, but he needed to stay in the hobo costume for the entire show.

"Let me just try it," said Emmett. He suddenly felt tired. Hadn't he uttered these same words years earlier – back when he talked Robinson Circus into letting him work as a hobo clown? How many times did he have to fight this battle? Long ago he'd accepted that he'd never be the artist he'd dreamed of being as a kid. So why was he fighting so hard for this hobo clown? Why risk his job?

Ringling's clowns worked in groups. The circus

had never used a clown who worked by himself. Despite this, Anderson said that he'd let Emmett remain as Weary Willie throughout the dress rehearsal – just the dress rehearsal. "Don't get your hopes up," Anderson said.

✦

Madison Square Garden was nearly dark. The circus's opening parade – called the "Spec," short for spectacular – had just ended. Glittering floats and fantastically dressed performers slowly circled the giant three-ring arena and then disappeared through the big double doors. Music from the brass band faded.

The lights lowered, and the audience hushed. Everyone expected the show to begin with the big cats. That was the usual opening act. People looked toward the giant black iron cage in the far ring, and they listened for the thrilling sound of roaring lions.

Instead, a spotlight suddenly flashed onto the center ring. Its brilliant light formed a pale halo around its edges. In that halo stood a man dressed in tattered clothes, a broom slung over his shoulder.

Emmett felt the sweat break out along his collar. "Willie," he said to himself – and he would remember this moment for the rest of his life, "this is the Big One. The world's biggest show in the world's biggest city." Emmett was about to do a routine that

The crowd in this photograph is standing outside Madison Square Garden in the 1920s.

would make him world famous. Of course, he had no way of knowing the future. He was just hoping that tomorrow he'd still have a job.

Willie stared at the spotlight. He lifted the broom from his shoulder and swept along the edge of the light, just as someone might sweep up spilled sugar. The circle became a little smaller. The clown, his sad face intent on his job, continued brushing at the light. With each stroke, the spotlight grew smaller and smaller. Finally only a tiny dot remained.

The audience was silent. They watched the dot of light, only an inch away from the sad clown's big floppy shoe. They weren't laughing, but Emmett could feel their eyes on him. He knew they were wondering: What will happen next?

Willie opened his tattered jacket. From deep inside one of its pockets, he pulled out a dustpan. He bent down and swept the tiny dot onto the pan.

For the first time, Willie seemed content. The sad-face hobo had a victory. He'd gotten rid of that pesky light. He slung the broom over his shoulder and turned to leave.

Suddenly, the spotlight flashed on again! Willie leaped backwards in surprise. The audience laughed. The light was big as ever. It blocked the path of the poor hobo.

Willie again lifted the broom from his shoulder and began sweeping the edge of the stubborn spotlight.

The lights went up around the big cat cage, and the show continued. When the audience's attention turned to the new act, Emmett strolled out of the ring.

It was a simple routine, but it went to the heart of Weary Willie's character. Emmett later described that character.

I am a sad and ragged little guy who is very serious about everything he attempts — no matter how futile or how foolish it appears to be. I am the hobo who found out the hard way that the deck is stacked, the dice 'frozen,' the race fixed and the wheel crooked, but there is always present that one tiny, forlorn spark of hope still glimmering in his soul which makes him keep on trying... [T]here must be a lot of people in this world who feel that way...who are down on their luck, have had disappointments and have maybe been pushed around by circumstances beyond their control...By laughing at me, they really laugh at themselves, and... this gives them a sort of spiritual second wind for going back into the battle.

After that dress rehearsal, Anderson found Emmett. He told the clown that he could stay in the hobo costume from now on. "You know, you're an artist," the manager said. When Emmett looked puzzled, Anderson added, "Even a clown can be an artist."

Whiteface clowns.

❖18❖

Death Comes To the Circus

It was July 6th, 1944. The day was hot. By noon, the tar that filled street cracks was sticky. But the heat didn't dampen anybody's excitement. Today the Greatest Show on Earth was in town – Hartford, Connecticut.

Long lines waited at the three ticket booths. At 1:00 P.M., the main tent opened. Almost 9,000 people crowded inside to see the three-ring circus.

Emmett sat by his trunk in clown alley. He pulled out Weary Willie's ragged costume and set out the clown make-up. He rubbed grease paint on his upper face and then rinsed the make-up sponge in the wash bucket beside his trunk. After rolling some putty into a ball, he pressed the ball onto his nose. He hoped the putty wouldn't melt in the heat.

At 1:45, Emmett heard the bugler and knew the show was about to start.

The first act featured wild animals – May Kovar and her 15 jaguars and leopards. Next came the Great Wallendas, the most famous highwire act in the world.

In the dressing room tent, Emmett heard the circus band playing a waltz. That was his cue to head over to the big tent. He and another clown were scheduled to stand under the high-wire act and hold out a little handkerchief, as if ready to catch a falling Wallenda.

Shortly after the Wallendas began their act, a few people near the main entrance smelled something burning.

A flame, small as a quarter at first, burned through the side of the tent. A police detective sitting near the top bleachers saw it. He didn't say anything because he believed that a circus worker would see the little fire and put it out. Other witnesses reacted the same way. No one said anything. No one put out the tiny fire.

The flame grew larger. A few seconds later, a pop vendor saw it and yelled, "Fire." Amazingly most people paid no attention. They were too interested in watching the Great Wallendas. Other people thought it was part of the show.

From the highwire, one of the Wallendas saw the flame and told the others to climb down. Merle Evans, the circus's bandleader, also noticed the fire. He stopped the band from playing the waltz and directed the musicians to play a march, "The Stars

and Stripes Forever." This march was an emer-
gency signal to circus people.

Now dressed as Weary Willie, Emmett heard the
band playing "The Stars and Stripes Forever." He
dropped his makeup and headed outside. From the
far end of the big top, he saw black smoke rising.

Emmett felt the blood drain from his face. The
audience was in there – children were in there!
Emmett tried to run, but Willie's big, floppy shoes
made running difficult. That's when he realized he
was carrying his wash bucket. But the fire was now
near the tent's roof, too far up for Emmett to throw
a bucket of water.

When the fire lapped onto the roof, the flames
moved rapidly across the tent's top, spreading along
the web of seams on the canvas. At that time, canvas tents were waterproofed with a mixture of
paraffin and gasoline. Consequently, the tent
burned like tissue paper.

Inside the tent, everyone could see the fire.
Some people were so stunned by the giant blaze
that they froze in their seats. Most people, however,
began to run.

From the outside, Emmett heard chairs crashing
inside the tent.

Many people naturally ran to the exit that they'd
used to enter – the main entrance. But that was
where the fire started, and where it was now most
intense. Some people tried escaping under the tent's

This photograph shows Emmett running with his water bucket toward the burning circus tent. It appeared in Life Magazine as the "picture of the week" and in other publications around the country and became one of the most famous images showing the Hartford fire.

sidewall, but it was anchored too tightly to the ground.

Parents tried to remain calm and lead their children to safety. Children, too, tried to remain calm. In school, they'd learned how to leave in an orderly fashion during a fire drill, but many adults were now panicking. Struggling to escape, people knocked each other down. In the pushing and shoving, many children were separated from their parents. Some fell and were trampled.

Emmett ran around the huge tent. Every exit was the same. Mass confusion. Some people – mothers, fathers, children – reached safety only to discover that their loved ones were missing. Many tried to run back inside to find them. One little girl stumbled outside and ran into Emmett. She was crying for her mother. When she turned back toward the tent, Emmett grabbed her. "Listen, honey – listen to the old clown," he said. "You go way over there in that victory garden and wait for your mommy. She'll come along soon."

This was the first and only time that Weary Willie ever spoke in public.

Years later, in his autobiography, Emmett would write, "The last I saw of her she was trotting over to the edge of the show grounds…I never learned if she found her mother, but it was a long time before I could stop dreaming about her."

The band continued to play. Evans hoped the music would calm the people, but the sound was barely heard over the screaming and the roar of the fire.

Chunks of canvas and aerial rigging began to fall. The melting paraffin rained down, a liquid fire, falling into people's hair, igniting cotton shirts and dresses. Skin and hair broiled. People escaping the blaze were on fire. One woman described the burnt arms of one little boy. They "looked like peanut butter," the woman said.

Near the entrance a tall stack of pop-bottle crates was on fire. The glass bottles melted and formed a giant puddle.

The exits clogged with hundreds of people struggling to get out. People tripped over pop bottles, chairs and each other. Piles of injured and burned people blocked exits. And still the crowds pushed forward, trying to escape. One man held onto his wife and child. The flood of people finally tore his wife from his grip. He watched as she was swept away with the crowd. She looked back at him and raised her hand. It was the last time he saw her alive.

Some people tried to help others who were too weak or injured to escape. One mother recalled that while she held her two-year-old son, the on-rushing crowd pinned her against a railing. A stranger helped pull her free. When the mother looked back, the strange man was helping other people.

The inferno raged inside the tent. People could no longer breathe the hot air. One man remem-

There were dozens of examples of heroism on the day of the terrible circus fire. Here is one: During the fire, a 13-year-old boy named Donald Anderson [shown here in front, left side] was trapped in the burning tent. He found a fishing knife in his pocket and cut a hole through the side of the tent. When Donald couldn't find his uncle outside, the boy tried to return through the hole he'd cut, but he couldn't. By now people were swarming through the newly made opening. The boy cut another hole in the tent and ran back inside to find his uncle. He found him, along with a lost little girl. Donald led both of them to safety. Dozens of people escaped due to his quick thinking.

People are still inside the Big Top, which was completely on fire when this photograph was taken.

bered, "The heat was unbearable. By this time, the howling and yelling were beyond description."

Standing outside, Emmett heard the screams, too. He remembered, "They all sounded like beaten dogs."

The center poles began to sway. The roof was now completely burned away. Some wires remained overhead, but when these finally burned, the swaying poles began to topple. Some smashed across the animal cages. Some crashed down on people trying to run.

Evans and his band continued to play as chunks of canvas fell around them. Suddenly the kettle-drums exploded from the heat. Evans told the band to run. No sooner did the musicians jump from the bandstand than one of the flaming tent poles, thick as a telephone pole, crashed near the stand.

Outside escaping people scrambled for the woods and the victory garden that bordered the circus grounds. The garden was full of children looking for their parents, and of parents looking for their children. Some people who escaped didn't stop running until they were home.

One man, who looked back at the fallen tent, remembered, "On the ground...I saw a number of people who were afire and were rolling themselves on the ground. I saw… people … whose clothing was afire, and under the stands I saw bodies on fire."

Many survivors recalled that the thing they'd remember all of their lives was the sound of screeching, wailing animals being burned alive when the tent finally fell. But there were no animals killed in the fire that day. What they heard were dying people.

The screams finally stopped. Now the long wail of fire trucks and ambulances filled the air. Emmett smelled the thick, horrid odor of burning flesh.

That evening he wandered out of the padroom and headed downtown to a hotel. He later wrote, "I walked past the ruins of the big top and saw some charred shoes and part of a clown doll lying on what had been the hippodrome track [center of the big top]. That moment was when the tension of the past hours broke over me in a wave, and I couldn't keep from crying any longer."

The fire killed 167 people. Sixty-seven were children under the age of 15. The Hartford fire was the worst circus disaster in history. It would be many weeks before the dead were identified. The body of one little girl was never identified. She was hardly burned at all. The only obvious injury was to the side of her face and neck. She had been trampled. All the other 166 bodies would be claimed, even the horribly burnt ones. During the next year, newspapers across the U.S. and Canada showed photographs of the dead girl's face. "Who knows this child?" the headlines said. But no one ever claimed her.

❖ 19 ❖

A Clown and a Murderer

By now Emmett was a circus star. The year of the Hartford fire, Ringling's spec – the opening parade with all the animals and performers – featured Emmett in the leading role. The spec showed the story of a hobo – Weary Willie – who fell asleep and dreamed that hundreds of animals and people, dressed in sparkling jewels and costumes, came to visit him. Of course, Willie finally woke up. The wonderful dream vanished, and Willie was once again a lonely hobo.

It had been more than 50 years since Ringling had singled out one performer to highlight in the spec. The circus gave him his own private sleeping room on the train. Everyone in the country knew Emmett's name. Weary Willie was the most famous clown in the world.

In 1950, the Ringling circus formed a partnership with Hollywood filmmakers for a big charity event in Los Angeles, California. One hundred and ten movie celebrities performed with the circus. Emmett created clown routines for three of the stars: Van Johnson, Bing Crosby and Frank Sinatra.

Shortly afterwards a movie agent talked to Emmett about doing a movie for the famous film studio owner, David O. Selznick.

Emmett had hoped to work in the movies, and here was his big chance. Selznick offered to pay Emmett a great deal of money. The studio owner had no idea what kind of movie was suited for a clown like Weary Willie. But Selznick believed Emmett's tens of thousands of fans would pay to see the famous personality in a movie.

For several weeks, Emmett waited at his hotel to hear from Selznick. The studio sent Emmett a weekly paycheck, although he didn't have a movie role. This made Emmett nervous. He was used to working two shows a day, rain or shine. He had never made money for doing nothing.

Finally Emmett asked permission to go to Chicago. The Ringling circus was scheduled to appear in the midwest town, and Emmett wanted to visit his circus friends. The studio agreed, but said that Emmett had to stay near a phone in case he was needed immediately in California. Emmett sat in his hotel and watched the train carrying The Big One arrive in Chicago. The sight of the wagons, animals and performers made him homesick for the circus. So much of his adult life, Emmett had been on the road, away from his family in Illinois. He still felt sad about the break-up of his marriage. He hardly knew his sons anymore. It was a lonely life. His only family was his circus friends. Emmett wondered why he'd ever imagined he wanted to leave and go to Hollywood.

On his third day in Chicago, Emmett received a message from his movie agent: "Take next plane to Los Angeles. Movie selected."

Selznick wanted Emmett for a movie called *The Fat Man*. Emmett was excited to read the movie's script. He would play a character named Ed Deets. But the more Emmett read of Deets and *The Fat Man* story, the more depressed he became. In the story, Deets murdered a dentist and nurse and then set fire to a truck with a man inside it. Deets then bought a circus with stolen money. To escape the police, Deets dressed as a clown. The studio wanted Emmett to use his famous Weary Willie costume for the movie clown.

The thought of a murderer hiding behind the character of Weary Willie made Emmett so sad that he couldn't sleep. He wanted very much to act in movies, but he worried about the effect that Willie's role in the movie would have on his young fans. Emmett had a firm rule: he never smoked or drank while wearing Willie's costume. He never did any-

This photograph and the other two on pages 104-105 show Emmett putting on make-up for his role as Ed Deets, a murderer who disguised himself as a whiteface clown in the movie, The Fat Man.

thing that cast the hobo in a bad light.

How would his fans – especially children – feel when they saw Weary Willie portrayed as a murderer? Emmett talked to some of his friends in Hollywood. One friend was Walt Disney who, like Emmett, had worked as a cartoonist in Kansas City. Disney agreed with Emmett. Don't use Willie for a villain. Another clown might be a villain but never the sad-face hobo.

Emmett had an idea. Ed Deets could hide behind the make up of a whiteface clown. The next day Emmett called his agent and told him the idea. The agent didn't like

The Fat Man was not popular with movie audiences. but another movie which featured Emmett, dressed as Weary Willie, was very popular. It was called The Greatest Show On Earth, *and was a story about Ringling Bros. and Barnum & Bailey Circus. The movie won "Best Picture" for 1952.*

it. It was too late to make script changes. Filming would begin in a few days. The film's producer and director also didn't like the whiteface idea.

Emmett knew that to some people Weary Willie was just grease paint, a ball of putty and some old tattered clothes. The hobo was just make-believe. But there were thousands of children who trusted in the goodness and gentleness of Willie. Emmett knew that. The fame and riches of Hollywood stardom were appealing things. But in the end they weren't enough. Not for Emmett. He simply couldn't sell out his sad-face clown.

Emmett told the studio people that he'd break his contract if they insisted on using Weary Willie as a murderer. Just when Emmett was ready to pack his suitcase and head back to Ringling, the studio called. The movie director asked Emmett to draw an example of a whiteface clown they could use instead of Weary Willie.

Emmett was so happy that he drew five different whiteface clowns. The studio picked one, and the filming of *The Fat Man* began the next day.

And that was how Emmett became a murderer — even if it was just pretend.

❧ 20 ❧

Endings and Beginnings

The year Emmett made *The Fat Man*, his mother
died. When he heard the news, he remembered
his boyhood years with his family. He remembered
his mother counting the coins from her sugar bowl
in Sedan, Kansas. He remembered her face when he
opened the package from the Landon School of
Cartooning back in Houston, Missouri. He remembered the first time she saw him perform as Weary
Willie.

After the show, he asked her, "Well, what did
you think of me out there?"

She shook her head and said, "You looked like
you didn't have one ounce of sense."

"That's good," said Emmett, "'cause I'm not
supposed to have any."

Both of them laughed. Oh, how they'd laughed,
Emmett remembered. Now she was gone, and he

felt a black knot where his heart should have been. During his years on the road, Emmett usually saw his mother only once a year. A short visit and then he was off again with the circus or some other performance. But he knew that whenever he needed to "go home" – when he was sick or sad – she was always there.

Not long after his mother's death, Emmett started writing his autobiography, *Clown*. Because he was famous, people wanted to read about his life. The book was made into a television movie and Henry Fonda, a famous actor, played the part of Emmett. But the death of his mother and the memories he had while writing *Clown* made Emmett realize how lonely he was. He lived a gypsy life. He never stayed more than a day or two in one town. Through the years he lost track of time. Day after day, city after city, he did the same routines over and over. Sure he loved his work. Seeing the joy on people's faces – especially children's faces – gave him deep satisfaction. But he was 56 years old, and he'd never owned his own home. He'd met presidents, kings and movie stars. But he hardly knew his own two sons. They were grown now with lives of their own.

In 1954, Emmett headed to New York City and Madison Square Garden. Emmett had performed with Ringling for 12 years. He was used to the excitement and dazzle of starting a new season. Even so, the opening at The Garden was always a big event. But that year – 1954 – ended up being one of the biggest years in Emmett's life.

One of the new acts in the circus was from Germany. "The Whirlwinds" was an acrobatic team. During dress rehearsal at The Garden, Emmett met one of the team members. Her name was Evi Gebhardt. She was young and pretty, and she laughed easily at Emmett's silly jokes.

Emmett saw Evi often. Although he liked her, he was very shy. In his life, he hadn't had luck with love. One day during the show, Emmett found enough courage to ask Evi if she'd have dinner with him at the cookhouse, the place where circus people ate. She surprised him by immediately saying yes.

All afternoon he worried about their meeting. Was she just starry eyed? Willie was famous, and Evi had never seen Emmett out of Willie's costume. Evi was so young. Emmett suddenly felt old. He wondered if she'd even recognize him without the hobo makeup.

She did. Later she'd say that she would have recognized him anywhere by his big, expressive eyes and bushy eyebrows.

Emmett knew why he'd had success as Weary Willie. In many important ways, Emmett and Willie were alike. Both knew the heartache of loss and loneliness. And yet both had the faith that someday things would get better.

And things did get better for Emmett. The loneliness ended when he met Evi. A romance grew between them. A year later they married. It was a big celebrity wedding. Photographers and reporters came. At the circus, the couple rode around the hippodrome in an open limousine.

Emmett and Evi's life together lasted for many years. But Emmett's life with the Ringling circus was coming to an end.

In the 1950s circuses everywhere were in trouble. Even the Ringling circus couldn't afford the heavy cost of tent shows and one-night stands. Moving 100 train cars of people and equipment day after day was expensive. Fewer people were coming to the circus, too. Television kept children and their parents at home. Why pay to see elephants and trapeze artists, when you could watch them free on television?

In 1956, Emmett and the rest of the Ringling circus headed out for a new season. They were in Pittsburgh in July when John Ringling North, the owner of the circus, ordered the show to pack up

Before going into the big top to watch the circus, the audience milled through the midway where the side shows provided a variety of entertainment. For more than a hundred years, until the mid 20th century, large crowds like this one attended circuses when they came to town.

and return to Sarasota, Florida. The season was only half over, but the circus was losing money.

And so Emmett's life with the circus came to an end. But for Weary Willie the end of the circus was just a beginning.

111

Toward the end of his career, Emmett told a reporter, "Willie and I have traveled a long, long way together since that day when he was born on my drawing board in Kansas City. A whole lot of it has been done on foot – tramping thousands of miles around the oval of the circus hippodrome, over and over again, nine to 15 times each show, twice a day rain or shine for the eight months of the tour plus more of the same at the winter indoor circus dates.

"The laughter of children is a sound no circus clown ever can forget. It sticks in his mind and he can still hear the echo warming his heart when he has put aside the makeup and the motley and quit trouping."

21

A Final Spotlight

From the farthest row in the New York Dodgers' stadium, the figure at homebase seemed as small as a pop bottle lid. But everyone knew him.

It was Weary Willie. Thousands of baseball fans watched him reach inside his tattered jacket pocket. He pulled out a whiskbroom and raised his arms. The umpire stepped aside. The Dodgers hitter and the Yankees catcher backed away. Willie stooped down and carefully brushed away the dirt from the base pad. With a flick of a finger, he removed the last grain of dirt and then motioned for the players to continue the game. The audience laughed and clapped their approval.

"Play ball," yelled the umpire.

For the first time in almost 40 years, Emmett didn't work for a circus. The Ringling circus had reorganized and headed back out the next spring to Madison Square Garden. But Weary Willie didn't join them. The Dodgers baseball team hired Emmett to be the team's mascot. He strolled around the baseball diamond pantomiming the actions of the players. He wandered around the audience, doing his old circus routines.

For the rest of his life, Emmett would perform in every kind of entertainment setting. He played at theaters and state fairs. He appeared on television and in movies. He made appearances in circuses, including the Shriner's Circus. Willie was also a success in world-famous nightclubs. For 13 seasons, he performed at Harrah's in Lake Tahoe, Nevada.

Emmett and Evi settled in Sarasota, Florida. They had two daughters. Emmett felt as if he'd been given a second chance. He was determined to make the most of it. Work was important to him, but now his family came first in his life. Evi and his daughters traveled with him when his various jobs took him away from Sarasota.

In 1962, Emmett and Evi bought a house. It was the first house Emmett had owned. He planted a garden and a few citrus trees. One was a grapefruit tree. He liked to pick a ripe yellow grapefruit, and tell the story about the time in Kansas City that he ate the strange, bitter fruit.

In the last few years of his life, Emmett received awards and special recognition from organizations around the country. In 1967, Gov. Ronald Reagan, on behalf of the state of California, honored Emmett in Sacramento, the state's capital.

That same year Emmett received an invitation from his birthplace, Sedan, Kansas. The town opened the Emmett Kelly Museum. Townspeople presented him with a large wooden key to the city. It was made of wood from his boyhood home. The next day Emmett performed his chalk talk routine for 700 students at the high school. The cartoons he drew that day still hang in the Kelly Museum.

In the year that Emmett turned 80 years old, he appeared with the Boston Opera Company. For a two-night stand, Weary Willie was in "The Bartered Bride." During the opera's carnival scene, Willie swept up a spot of light and brushed it into a dustpan. Just when he thought his job was complete, the light appeared again. No matter how hard he tried he couldn't make that spotlight disappear.

How many times had he performed that routine? A thousand? Maybe more. Hardly anyone in the audience had not seen that old routine. But still they loved it. There was something both sad and funny about it. Something that reminded them of themselves.

On March 28, 1979, "The Greatest Show On Earth" opened at Madison Square Garden. It was the 109th circus season. The Ringling circus had changed. Although it once employed 1,000 people, most had worked as laborers who packed, moved and set up the massive tents. Now the circus hired 225 people, and the show never appeared in tents. Instead the circus was booked throughout the year in arenas around the country. In Sarasota, still headquarters for Ringling, the circus operated a museum and a school to train new circus clowns. In 1973, the Ringling museum created an exhibit about clowns. The exhibit was dedicated to Emmett Kelly, "The World's Funniest Clown."

The Garden was still a big event. All morning long on that chilly Wednesday the roustabouts put up the aerial rigging and laid out the three big rings.

Eleven hundred miles south in Sarasota, Emmett was finishing breakfast in the kitchen. Just last December he celebrated his 80th birthday. Every one in Sedan, Kansas, signed a birthday card and mailed it to him. He sent back a thank-you note.

Emmett refused to retire, but these days he rarely went too far from home. Willie's tattered costume still hung in a special closet in Emmett's house. It was Willie's only suit. With a few repairs, Willie had worn it for more than 40 years. The next Monday, Emmett was scheduled to perform at the Robarts Sports Arena in Sarasota. He was also scheduled to do a short charity film with Tony Bennett, the singer.

Evi and one of her relatives from Germany were in the kitchen, too. Evi and Emmett had been married for 24 years. "Happiness," Emmett had recently told a reporter, "has come to me late in my life."

After finishing his breakfast, Emmett took out the garbage and said he would pick up the newspaper in the front yard. After a while, when he didn't return, Evi looked outside. Emmett was lying in the grass.

Later that day at The Garden, the circus announcer interrupted the first performance. The hippodrome was dark except for a single spotlight in the center ring.

"Shortly after 10 o'clock this morning," the announcer said, "Emmett Kelly died of a heart attack at his home in Sarasota."

There was a moment of silence for Emmett and the sad-face clown. And then the spotlight disappeared.

Circus Language ~ A Glossary

Big Top. The main circus tent in which the audience watched the performers.

Clown Alley. The dressing tent or area where clowns put on their costumes and makeup.

First of May. A new or first-season performer. The name came from the traditional schedule of a circus. Except for the circuses that operated in the warm climates of the south, most shows began their 40-week season during the first week in May.

Equestrian director. The person in charge of the entire circus performance and all the performers.

Hippodrome. The center area under the Big Top where the circus performances and parade occur.

Hold back. Circuses used this system of keeping one-week salary from each performer until the end of the tour. This helped insure that performers stayed with the show until the final performance of the season. It also meant that everyone had some money to get back home.

118

Joey. Another name for "clown." The name comes from the famous British clown, Joseph Grimaldi (1779-1837), who performed in theaters and music halls. He worked in white-face, similar to the illustration on page 118.

Padroom. Dressing room for circus performers.

Ringmaster. The person who stood in the middle of a ring of trained horses.

Sideshow. This was a cluster of attractions outside the Big Top. It sometimes included dozens of variety shows. These might feature sword swallowers, magicians, belly dancers, contortionists and weight lifters.

Spec. Spectacular. This was the big pageant under the Big Top in which all circus performers paraded in front of the audience.

The Garden. Madison Square Garden. For many years this was the first show of the circus season for Ringling Bros. & Barnum Bailey Circus. For this reason, circus performers adopted the expression, "See you at The Garden," when saying good bye to each other.

Trouper. A performer who is dependable, uncomplaining, and hard-working.

Truck show. A small circus, such as the Haag Circus (called Hog Show by circus people). Truck shows, also called dog and pony shows, used trucks to move from town to town. Big circuses transported their equipment and performers in trains. Today circuses travel by air.

J.L. Wilkerson, a native of Kentucky, now lives in Kansas City, Missouri. A former teacher, Wilkerson has worked as a writer and editor for more than 25 years. She is an award-winning writer whose essays and articles have appeared in professional journals and popular magazines in the United States and Great Britain. She is the author of several regional history books for adults. Wilkerson also has written children's books, including other biographies for Acorn Books' The Great Heartlanders Series.

Information about Emmett Kelly's life and times is available through these resources:

Ballantine, Bill. "Emmett in the Kitchen." Showfolks of Sarasota, Inc. (An International Alliance of Circus Artists and Executives) 1980 Yearbook.

Emmett Kelly Museum in Sedan, Kansas.

Fox, Charles Philip and Tom Parkinson. *The Circus In America*. Country Beautiful, Waukesha, Wisconsin, MCMLXIX (1959).

Kelly, Emmett, with F. Beverly Kelley. *Clown*. Prentice-Hall, Inc., New York, 1954.

O'Nan, Stewart. *The Circus Fire, a True Story*. Doubleday, New York, 2000.

Verney, Peter. *Here Comes the Circus*. Paddington Press LTD, New York, 1978.

Culhane, John. *The American Circus, an Illustrated History*. Henry Holt and Company, New York, 1989.

Hoh, LaVahn G. and William H. Rough. *Step Right Up! – The Adventure of Circus in America*. Betterway Publications, Inc., 1990.

These and other sources were used during the research of *Sad-Face Clown: Emmett Kelly*.

PRAISE FOR
THE GREAT HEARTLANDERS SERIES

"Although the books are clearly designed with an eye toward the classroom...they are well-written and interesting enough to capture children's imaginations on their own."

Omaha World Herald, 10/12/98.

"The inviting formats, easy-to-read texts, and black-and-white photographs and sketches will draw both reluctant readers and report writers."

American Library Association, *School Library Journal*, 3/99

"Acorn Books is doing a great service for eight-to twelve-year olds by publishing their attractive ~ Great Heartlanders Series...The care that Acorn Books takes with its books is evident. They are filled with informational maps or diagrams and include black and white photographs of many of the books' subjects."

Nebraska Library Commission ~The Nebraska Center for the Book, *NCB News*, Spring, 2000.

"Acorn Books has launched an outstanding biography series for young readers called `The Great Heartlanders'."

Midwest Book Review, "Children's Bookwatch," 11/98.

ACORN BOOKS
THE GREAT HEARTLANDERS SERIES

Making history an active part of children's lives.

You can find this book and other Great Heartlanders books at your local fine bookstores.

For information about school rates for books and educational materials in THE GREAT HEARTLANDERS SERIES, contact

Acorn Books
THE GREAT HEARTLANDERS SERIES
7337 Terrace
Kansas City, MO 64114-1256

Other biographies in the series include:

Scribe of the Great Plains: Mari Sandoz
Champion of Arbor Day: J. Sterling Morton
A Doctor to Her People: Dr. Susan LaFlesche Picotte
From Slave To World-Class Horseman: Tom Bass
Frontier Freighter: Alexander Majors
Fighting Statesman: Sen. George Norris
American Illustrator: Rose O'Neill
Story of Pride, Power and Uplift: Annie T. Malone

Additional educational materials in THE GREAT HEARTLANDERS SERIES are

* Activities Books   * Celebration Kits
* Maps   * "Factoid" Bookmarks
* Posters

Acorn Books also distributes dozens of books and videos that relate to The Great Heartlanders biographies.

To receive a free Great Heartlanders catalog and a complete list of series books, other regional books and videos, and educational materials, write or call Acorn Books.

Toll Free: 1-888-422-0320+READ (7323)

www.acornbks.com